F

&

Nonsense

Creations from a Broken Mind

Bryony Best

Paperback: 978-1-7392860-6-4

Cover design chosen by: Bryony Best

Editor: Lucie O'Donnell

www.bryonybest.com

Dedication Page

I dedicated this book to my fellow warriors who also have walked the path of darkness.

Pages

Blossom

Big pink flowers combined to make a tree, beautiful from a distance or where ever you may see.

They look good, smart, and respectable, cool as a summer scene, similar to a bunch of friends leaning, and holding each other up as they lean. And in the sun they smell, sparkle and beam. Then they begin to die and fall softly like a handkerchief, slowly they drift to the ground and huddle to make a wreath.

Eventually the tree is left bare and the blossom dies, but like all good things it must come to an end. And it is no scene to anyone as it rots and bends.

Baffled

If I am dead, but death is me.

Dead or death I cannot become.

So who, or what could I be?

October Morning

The trees blow viciously with a sharp, cold wind, sending shivers down my spine as though they were sinned.

The whirly winds whistle, and the fog never lifts, like the miserable outlook of a winters drift.

A dull grey sky, with no birds that fly.

No animals in sight, due to shivering frost bite.

When all seems lost and the darkness is near, a ray of light shines, releasing the fear.

A fight begins between light and night, but the light is stronger, bigger, and bright.

As the sun breaks through the clouds, the whistling stops, the trees end to rock, the fog dissolves, and the animals reappear.

Now the darkness is anything but near.

Gun

A destructive friendship

I was not really shopping for a gun, but this one was similar to one that I saw in my mind's eye.

It was small, and looked better than the others. Plus it was solid, just like me.

The gun was cheap and we had a hectically wonderful time ahead of us, like laughs, danger, and many vacations.

At first I was shocked at how easily the gun fit into my life, and it made living so much more enjoyable.

Eventually the sparkle I had first seen in the gun began to disappear, and what remained was an uglier and harsher gun.

The gun did not feel the same in my hand as it did before, and instead the gun became what it had always been.

The gun was an enemy.

Cycle

Lions and tigers patrolling the land, no music playing as they are their own band.

The beat of the drum in the jungles mouth, which rattles like a python hanging from a tree.

The birds flying high like a perfect kite, dancing on the wind and twirling in the sky.

The hippos in the water moving graciously like a ballerina, echoing strength, and years of existence.

The beautiful colours of a parrot up above, like a flying rainbow or a smoking dove.

The noises so strange that they hold you, frozen as you calculate the sounds.

Monkeys in the trees, a swinging bush, with wildebeests by the watering hole wetting their snouts.

No danger is feared as they all become one, the hunter, the hunted, Mother Nature as they run.

The breeze on their face, the flies on their back, and the never ending knowledge that prey could attack.

The sun in her glory that gives them their home, but she who shall take it, when Miss. Rain never shows.

The jungle turns to dust and home begins to rot, no watering hole, no ballerina, just the unknown.

Days and weeks watching your young grow weak, times are tough, the safari is bleak.

The vultures arrive just in time, the dinner bell has rung.

Fair

What is being fair?

Is it when you give someone a choice, a chance, or a warning in advance of things to come?

Is it fair that for someone to win, someone will have to lose?

When a man wins over the woman he loves, does another lose their lover, mother, or sister?

If a man at the front selects the last eggs is it fair the person behind will go without?

Is it fair that in order to learn and grow we must endure pain?

Is it fair that some people get things much easier than others?

Are you fair?

I am not!

We should look after our world the way it takes care of us.

Everything is living, and it all has a purpose, otherwise it wouldn't be here.

I am here to help others, when the time is right.

Do not push, for the day will come and peace will be my gift.

I've Never

I have never made a snowman or tried to learn to surf.

I have never picked an apple, or grown something in the earth.

I have never followed a butterfly just to see where it goes.

I have never sat and caressed my feet, counting one or more of my toes.

I have never just sat by the sea and watched the world go by.

I have never known it wasn't wrong, each time I've told a lie.

I've never run as I did as a child and felt as free as a bird.

I've never paid attention to a siren, or wondered where it's being lured.

BUT

I have told a lie, and wished I would die.

I have cried in pain, and envied other's gain.

I have neglected my family and my friends, to go off on a drinking bend.

I have been rude and chose to smoke, and I have spoken before I should have spoke.

I have thrown rubbish on the floor; but I won't go on for there is so much more.

When I next have a spare day, I shall throw on my shoes where they lay, hang up my worries and forget about my flaws, and try one of my many things that I have never done before.

Melt Down

Everything needs to breakdown, to be reborn.

What niggles at your soul at night?

What holds you back from the truth?

Acceptance is the answer!

Once this is done, the soul can release any trapped energy and move on.

To build and grow you will need a solid foundation to be laid, and one must slay old demons.

A fresh slate is needed to start a new path, allowing the release of your heartache.

And from the ashes a phoenix is born.

Delirium

When shadows appear and the sun is lost, we empty our secrets and swim in vain.

As our blood turns against us and recoils at a stare, we find comfort in hate and allies in enemies.

Instead of growing we deplete, recalling days lost to the now.

We use victories as stories and plans as hopeless dreams on a ship, wreaked within the storm.

Beauty is no longer depth but cosmetic, and not in the beholders eye.

We no longer question the reason we die, because the how and when are replaced with; if only.

We are the ones who should be replaced.

Rise Up

Similar to a drop of rain falling into the ocean, or a stone tumbling down a mountain side. Rise up.

If struck by lightning between the sounds of thunder, while silence overtakes all existence like the day is claimed by the night. Rise up.

When the unlikely becomes present and the impossible lingers, like a fly inside your mind sending ripples into your brain. Rise up.

Waves crashing into you from either side, above, below, left, and right. Rise up.

Powers that erode and chip away your minerals of hope, joy, and wonder. Leaving you a victim to the sea and her never ending thirst. Rise up.

If you are drifting without direction, aims or plans. Ensuring all is a gift rather than to risk disappointment, which taste like battery-acid laced on the tongue. Rise up.

If I cut out my tongue do I win?

Rise up.

Fire

As heat washes over me, like rocks of ice sending dampness to my insides.

Pounding and racing, burning with need.

Hungry for one thing, like a lion in the wild with his prey in sight.

Reason and rationality elopes, similar to a runaway child on a highway with their thumb raised for a lift.

The present is lost as time stands still, yet time flies faster than a bullet.

Feelings going wild similar to a teenage girl, twitching breasts, with a pulsating heartbeat between my legs.

Reality

Why there are voices in my head, like shadows are in the daytime when there is no rain?

No need for shelter for this is not reality; truth can only to be found in small moments.

Moments that cannot be caught, faked or stolen.

For they are real, unlike me. I am a reflection, a glimmer, an echo in time.

Who shall speak of me in time to come?

Will dreams be reversed, offering nightmares to be solved?

Gold will pour out of our eyes like tears of a newborn baby.

As grass grows down and the sky stretches.

While others are killed to come, and others are born to leave.

Who are we to judge reality?

Whose reality, for it's not mine?

Alcohol

Sickness is not my friend, yet it longs to be near me.

I fear it and loathe it, yet lack of respect causes the closeness.

As it tickles my insides and strokes my face.

It is not my enemy, for it has been let in by me.

Welcomed, pampered, door open, and tea is on the side.

As the kettle boils offering invitations to all, not my invitation but still they are signed by me.

My mind becoming confused and offering a white flag, for it cannot bear no more.

Take my money, family, and job for they are nothing without wellbeing.

Take a seat, for I shall stand and fight, like a gladiator.

Dark Liquid

You have been good, you have been a needed friend, but now you're the reason I am going around the bend.

It was always you who could make me smile, even if only for a short while.

When I was upset, it was you I would choose to tell, you were the only one who could ring my bell.

You have helped me cope with the long harsh days, keeping all my worries and troubles at bay.

You were my friend, family and foe, my saviour who saved me when I was low.

Now you have changed, or is it me?

Why has this happened, and how could it be?

What was once mellow, nice, and all things spice, is now nasty and mean and not so serene.

Vile and violent are the key words, she is no longer on the level, but is an evil twisted devil.

To not be in control or know what is going on, when I wake up confused in bed, with an empty memory weighing down in my head.

Broken Mind

I walk around the mountain feeling a bitter cold, as my legs start to ache and my body feels old.

Similar to a car needing a service and a new oil change, my future is ahead but it is still out of range.

Giant rocks in my path and stones in my shoes, breadcrumbs on the floor act as shiny new clues.

Keep Going. The light is shining and the gates are near, any moment now they will show and appear.

Rain falls to slow me and blind my twisted view, with a cold so deathly and hands that turn blue.

A flicker of hope arrives as a robin flown by, a star and a twinkle to light up the sky.

Silence turns against me and twists my mind's eye, a darkness upon me that taunts; you may die!

Weakness is all over me like a glorious coat, a rocking of madness or am I afloat?

No one is behind me, or walking this way, a hologram in the distance waving from the bay.

Broken may be my mind, influenced and torn, a prick in my finger like a poisonous thorn.

Dancing in the moonlight and smiling at the sky, for madness or not, I am still alive!

As the days are bleak and my mind grows weak, I pray for the lady who cries in the sky, to help my home grow and repair what's not whole.

I hear water splashing and others in the tree but when I look up I am alone, it is sadly just me.

Something happens and the bangs are too loud, the gentle lady is crying she is wearing her cloud.

My safety is breeched and I fear I might die, I hit my head and I am gone; Goodbye.

Am I in heaven as I open my eyes?

The weather is hot but she has dried her eyes. I take another look and my waterhole is full, the sun is shining and the world has not been destroyed.

Mother Nature has started again................

Weakness

You are ugly as sin and I hate your face, the winner of disgust, now take your place.

You have fallen so far and it is your cross to bare, no one ever said that life would be fair.

You dance with the devil and you pop your pills, your future is decided your fate is sealed.

Nameless faces and strangers in the crowd, a thunderstorm brews under your cloud.

Pain, torment, and emptiness inside, you are to blame, no one can deny.

It's not fair, but who cares?

Not God, Spirit, or the powers above will spare your soul, you must pay a toll.

Keep your empty promises to be a better soul, your lies are only fit for a toilet roll.

Acid and spite shoot from your tongue, you can't blame everything on when you was young.

A choice has been made, your tale has been told, but you can change before you are old.

Grey

To live in the grey is a merky time, life is rarely good and barley just fine.

Decisions and choices have to be made; the mask that I wear is simply a facade.

Like a sheep in line to be cut limb from limb, I am a shadow crying into the din.

Shady corners similar to the ones in my mind, a sickness has hold of me, and my bones it will grind.

I am fatty mince meat that has been through the mill, I will be consumed until it has killed.

How can I walk in the shadows but dance in the sun?

I can sprint my fastest but the darkness still comes.

I am rotten to my core and my fight is done, there is nowhere to hide and nowhere to run.

God

I have fallen so far down, that I am deep underground.

A vacuum of silence where there is no sound.

The only voices are the ones in my head which whisper in my ear that they wish I was dead.

I created the monster and it has been overfed, fresh cuts, it's happiest after I have bled.

My body is its nourishment while it feasts on my soul, my evil deeds feed it an overflowing bowl.

A coffee bean floating in milk that's now sour, an outlaw with a gun sitting on the tower.

Aiming a barrel directly at my face.

BANG.

I am gone.

I'm released from this place.

Darkness

I sleep in the dark but I walk in the sun.

I return to the shadows and drink my rum.

A bottle or two to numb the pain, to relax my senses, and quiet my brain.

Too many thoughts inside my head, a good reason to avoid my empty bed.

Surrounded by mongrels to distract my chain of thoughts, I sit at the head of the table of my sinful court.

I pass judgment and place the blame, with tedious evidence to prove my claim.

I am the judge and jury as I wear my crown, vomiting my parade all over town.

Who am I to judge?

Weep

As I sit in my room and weep, wishing I could be a sheep.

Following others around where ever they may go, I could fall into line and walk with the flow.

If I quack like a duck and laugh when they do, will I become just like you?

If I was quiet as a mouse watching others walk by, would I be still and no longer cry?

A wolf in sheep's clothing but I could not hide for long, as they would soon notice that I did not belong.

I can't quack, and I never could follow.

To sit still is beyond me, I need to be free.

We are NOT the same.

These poems were composed during Bryony's darkest days, battling alcohol and drug addiction while suffering with mental health issues.

"Never give up. Nothing last forever, the good or the bad"

Bryony Best

Final Message to the Reader

I would like to thank you from the bottom of my heart for purchasing and reading this book. Please do consider reading my other publications.

I do ask, that you please take the time to leave a review on the site where you purchased this book and do also add your review to Goodreads - if you have an account with them.

Please upload a picture with your review to your social media platforms as this will help others to find my book.

Website – www.bryonybest.com

Sign up to my newsletter for rewards and exclusive discounts.

Twitter - @bryony_best

Instagram - @bestbryony

Facebook – The Girl from Pompey

Tik Tok - @bryonybest

Bryony Best

AUTHOR BIO

Bryony Best was born and raised in Portsmouth, United Kingdom. Currently residing in South Wales with her fiancé and her much loved Chihuahua dog named Luna. Bryony works as a Holistic Therapist, Author, and Life Coach. She lives a happy life of mindfulness and wellbeing. Bryony has previously published five books, and her aim is to become a full-time writer.

(The Girl from Pompey: Discovering the Key to Happiness and Fulfilment) Published - 2021

(The Girl from Pompey: Conversations with the Dead!) Published – 2022

(The Girl from Pompey: Bloodshed in the Hampshire Cabin) Published - 2023

(A Healing Journey: Healing the Body, Mind, and Spirit) Published – 2023

(The Girl from Pompey: Escaping the Rat Race) Publish 2024

Bryony's inspiration to share her stories with the world is to shine a light on mental health, and trauma healing. Since releasing her books, Bryony has become an advocate for mindfulness and wellbeing. Bryony delivers wellbeing workshops and courses for aspiring authors.

Printed in Great Britain
by Amazon

48165688R00020